D0479521

WATERCOLORS

SpiceBox

First published in 2010 by
SpiceBox™
12171 Horseshoe Way.
Richmond, BC Canada
V7A 4V4
www.spicebox.ca

This edition published in 2010.
Text Copyright © Philip Berrill 1996
Written and Illustrated by Philip Berrill
All rights reserved.

No part of this publication may be reproduced,
stored in a retrieval system, or transmitted in any
form or by any means, electronic, mechanical,
photocopying, recording or otherwise, without
the prior written permission of the publishers and
copyright holders.

ISBN 10: 1-926906-30-X
ISBN 13: 9781894905930

Printed in China

Photography by Peter Raymond, Southport

Contents

It is with sadness that we write that Mr. Philip Berrill passed away at the end of 2009 after suffering a number of health related setbacks.

Despite the loss to the art world and potential art students everywhere, it is with pride that the SpiceBox team continues to share his legacy of art with you. We first published Philip's books in 2004, and due to their popularity continue to reprint them every year. We have updated this edition in order to keep the books fresh and current, but we have made as few changes as possible to the lessons in creating art that Philip has left with us. We hope you enjoy his instruction and words of encouragement.

Editor

About the Artist

Philip Berrill (1945-2009) was a professional artist, art tutor, lecturer and author whose techniques and methods of learning to paint are taught and enjoyed worldwide.

From the age of three, when he used a sprayer to Whitewash his father's tomato plants, until his passing, Philip believed art could transform the world. Under the tutelage of Welsh artist, John Sullivan, Philip held his first one-man exhibition at the age of 18. By age 28, a major exhibition of his work was held at the Liverpool University, and as a result, Philip was able to realize his dreams of becoming an established, professional artist.

He launched his very successful art classes using his special approach to teaching, sketching and painting, and then went on to develop his worldwide correspondence art courses. His highly sought-after painting holiday courses were held in locales such as Great Britain, Rome, Venice, Florence and Paris, and Philip was also invited to lecture and demonstrate painting on sea cruises around Europe the USA and Dubai. It was during this time in his career that Philip earned the nickname "The Flying Artist".

Philip's love and enthusiasm for sketching and painting was infectious. He believed that art should be for everyone and that you are never too young or too old to start sketching. Philip's students have ranged from 10 to 80 years of age and he enjoyed passing on his enthusiasm and knowledge of how to sketch and paint to people from all walks of life and almost every background imaginable. Philip's sketching and painting courses and techniques are designed to be suitable for people of all abilities and all ages.

This book is intended to cover a range of mediums, techniques and subjects to introduce you to the joy and pleasure of sketching and painting. Each book has been beautifully presented in a high quality laptop easel with all the materials you will need to get started painting and drawing. The compact form and portability of each kit will allow you the freedom and spontaneity to capture each moment of inspiration the way Philip demonstrated with his own work. We hope that you will enjoy the kits and that they will assist you in your journey of sketching and painting.

Right *Author, artist, lecturer, Philip Berrill*

Below *Watercolor of the Piazza San Marco and the Palazzo Ducale*

Introduction

How often have you wished that you could paint? From the earliest times, man has drawn and painted. From cave paintings by primitive man in France and Spain to the stylized and beautiful decorative art of the Egyptians; from Byzantine mosaics to great works of the Italian Renaissance such as the Mona Lisa and the Last Supper by Leonardo da Vinci, painting transcends generations, nationalities and ages. Indeed, art transcends language, race or political boundaries and is as much of a pleasure to create as it is to view. Pictures and artwork surround us; they are on the greeting cards that we send and on the book covers we read, on food packages, and fabric designs, pictures are everywhere! They can be funny, serious, moving, calming, challenging or reassuring; pictures, drawings and paintings are part of our everyday life. No wonder so many people say "I wish I could paint." My message to you is: if you want to, you can!

There is no need to be apprehensive about painting. Picasso said at age fifteen he drew and painted like the Italian Master Raphael, but that it took him many more years to learn to paint like a child. If you watch young children, the moment they can pick up a pencil, marker or crayon, they are determined to make marks, to draw and scribble. Quite quickly, by the age of three to four, they start to draw and color the things they see around them, giving their pictures a wonderful degree of expression.

Painting allows a nearly unlimited range of styles and forms. Watercolors especially provide a marvelous means of producing detailed, precise or delicate pictures — or in contrast, bold, quickly painted studies. For example, landscapes capturing the atmospheric effects of rain, mist and sunlight are difficult to obtain in any other medium. Apart from landscapes, watercolors lend themselves to the painting of all subjects including seascapes, still life, portraits, animals and flowers, yet allow for artist's developing of their own style.

Watercolors are an ideal medium to paint for other reasons as well; they require a minimum amount of equipment and involve little, if any, mess. Another nice aspect of watercolor painting is that you don't need a separate room or studio; the materials take up only a small amount of space and can be used on a kitchen or dining room table. They are equally convenient outside or for using indoors.

If you are a beginning painter looking for that boost of confidence and good advice, you will find this book and kit of supplies are the perfect way to get started exploring this exciting art. Or, if you already sketch or paint, I hope this kit will help to renew your interest, advance your skills, or introduce you to a medium that you may not have tried before, and inspire you with new ideas. I also hope that the compact format of this kit will encourage you to take your painting outdoors and enjoy your pastime in a variety of environments.

People often ask me if painting is a gift only a few possess. My answer to that is no, I firmly believe that the art of being able to sketch and paint is born in everyone. Some people say to me "I would love to paint but I can't draw a straight line." It comes down to motivation. The moment anyone says "I would love to paint," I can assure them that following the right advice and with a little regular practice, they will be able to. I have proven this over and over again with many people of all ages and from all backgrounds. They have taken my advice, followed the demonstrations and techniques, and have become proficient artists in their own right, often producing high-quality work, amazing themselves, their family, and friends. Many have had the great pleasure of seeing their work accepted for exhibition, and have sold paintings. Some have even had their own solo exhibitions. Whether painting solely for your own pleasure and enjoyment, or striving to exhibit, everyone can enjoy the art of painting.

Tom Jones was paralysed in an accident. Philip taught Tom to paint using his mouth.

Materials For Watercolor Painting

During the past thirty to forty years there have been many exciting changes and developments in artists' materials and equipment, more so than the previous three centuries. This has been largely due to advances in the science of color chemistry which have had a significant effect on the materials an artist uses and have opened up new avenues undreamt of by artists of previous generations. The artist now has water soluble pencils, nylon brushes, acrylic and synthetic paints, in addition to the traditional watercolors, oil paints and pastels at their disposal. A number of the modern developments benefit today's watercolor painter.

Watercolor painting does not need to be expensive. One can start a sketch on the back of an envelope. Art material manufacturers are conscious of both quality and the artist's pocket. They provide top quality materials known as Artists quality, where price is given secondary importance to quality, but ever conscious of the limited finances of many painters and students, they also produce excellent modestly priced paints, brushes and materials.

The Winsor and Newton **artists quality** watercolors and their Cotman watercolors and brushes are fine examples of both qualities. I will describe several ranges of materials within this book for your guidance. A simple rule should be, buy the best art materials you can afford. Painting is a very personal experience and you will find that you come to have favourite brushes, paper and equipment.

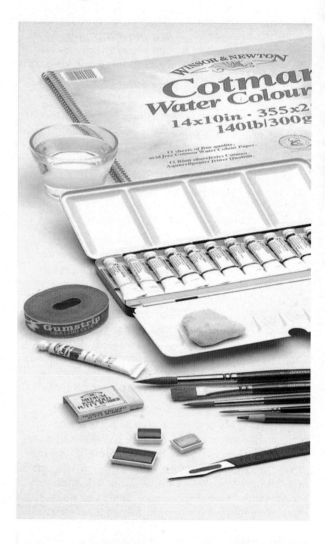

Brushes

It is important to have good quality brushes. The tip of your paint brush is the most important thing between you and your painting. Your paint brushes should be treated with respect and be well cared for, and in return they will give you good service. Your brush should feel like an extension of your fingers. There are ranges of natural hair brushes. Traditionally sable brushes, especially Kolinsky sable, found in the Winsor and Newton series seven range, have been considered by many artists as the best, but the scarcity of high quality sable hair has led to the development of nylon and synthetic brushes.

The brushes come in two main shapes, round and flat. The round brushes are usually graded from 0000 to 24 depending on the range. The larger and medium brushes are for general painting and the smaller round brushes are for detail. The flat wash brushes are used for applying large, broad washes of color to your painting. They are normally graded by width from 1/8 in (3mm) to 1½ in (38mm) or wider.

Paint

Watercolors are a finely ground mixture of pigment, gum arabic (a water soluble gum from the acacia tree), glycerine (which helps keep the colors moist) and wetting agents (which help the paint flow freely). The paint, when diluted with water on the palette and applied as a wash by brush onto the surface of the paper, has a translucent quality which is a feature of the medium. Paints such as oils or acrylics are essentially opaque and white paint is mixed with the other colors to lighten them. The pure watercolorist uses no white paint: water is used to lighten the color and the whiteness of the paper reflects the light through the wash.

Watercolors are available in three forms; tubes, pans or half pans. Pans and half pans are small, square or rectangular dishes of solid color. Tubes are more convenient for studio use. Color can be squeezed on to the palette from the tube and the color released with a wet brush. Dried out, the paint can be moistened easily with water. Pans of color are convenient for outdoor work because they usually come in sets and are easily portable. Pans are slightly less soluble than tube colors and a little gentle rubbing with the brush is needed to release the colors.

Watercolor Paper

The paper the watercolor painter uses is very important. I recommend that you use one of the papers specially made for watercolor painting. Cartridge paper, while ideal for drawing, is too thin for watercolor painting and can waver and distort when water is applied to it. Watercolor paper is either made from a wood pulp, from sustainable forests, or from a cotton rag pulp. Both have characteristics all their own. Wood pulp paper is a little less expensive than cotton rag paper. Experiment with both to find the paper which suits you best.

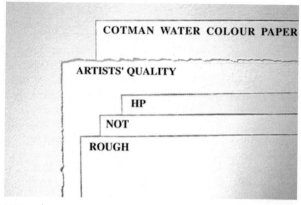

Watercolor paper

Watercolor paper surfaces

Watercolor paper varies in thickness and surface texture. Both offer the artist different options for painting on. The surfaces are **HP** (Hot Pressed): this is a very smooth surface ideal for detailed work; **Rough**: this has a very pronouced surface and is ideal for bold, free flowing subjects; **Not** paper, sometimes referred to as **CP** (Cold Pressed): this is not rough and not smooth but midway between, and a very popular surface for many watercolor painters. It is the one I suggest you try first. While watercolor paper is traditionally white, it is possible to obtain **tinted paper**. The colored paper has many uses and I will refer to these in a later chapter.

Spiral bound watercolor paper

Watercolor paper thickness

The weight of watercolor paper is calculated by how much 500 full size Imperial sheets (a ream) of paper weighs. The thicker the sheet, the heavier the paper. Popular watercolor weights are 90 lb (l90gsm), 140 lb (300gsm) and 300 lb (640gsm). I recommend that you work on 140 lb (300gsm) paper with a "**Not**" surface. This is readily obtainable from art stores and art shops in sheet and watercolor sketch book form. Sheets of watercolor paper come in imperial size 30 x 22 in (762 x 559 mm). One sheet folded and cut into four will provide paper for four medium sized watercolor paintings. Many years ago paper was handmade and such paper can still be obtained today. However, in recent years machinery has enabled the manufature of mould-made watercolor paper. Winsor and Newton produce two excellent watercolor papers, a cotton rag Artists Watercolor Paper and their Cotman Watercolor Paper.

Both are of fine quality, with the Cotman paper being the less expensive. These popular papers can be obtained in sheet, sketch book, or block form. You can cut the sheets to whatever size that you require. The watercolor sketch books are usually spiral bound. The watercolor blocks come as a number of sheets mounted on a stiff backing board and gummed at the sides of the block. The paper on the blocks, if the painting is carried out on the block, does not require stretching. The sheet is carefully removed at the end of the painting. The technique of stretching is described in the next section. Watercolor painting boards are also available. The board has a sheet of watercolor paper glued to the surface and can be cut to any size you require.

Stretching paper

Watercolor washes can cause paper to wave and distort when applied to the paper. Artists overcome this by stretching or pre-shrinking their watercolor paper to eliminate the likelihood of the paper wavering. For this you will require a wooden drawing board, or piece of ply board, measuring not less than 18 x 14 in (457 x 356 mm). The board needs to have a matt wooden finish, not varnished or painted white, as the gummed tape will not stick to these surfaces. Cut a sheet of watercolor paper at least 2 in (50 mm) smaller than the board. Run the paper under the cold water tap soaking both sides thoroughly. Let the surplus water drain off the paper surface, then lay the wet paper on your board. Use a clean, dry tissue to wipe a ½" (13mm) edge of the paper along all four sides. The edge should look matt, the wetness of the rest of the paper should glisten. Cut strips of your 1 in (25 mm) wide gummed paper and wet them. Stick half the width of each strip onto the edges of the paper and half the width firmly on to the board. Let the gummed paper dry for five minutes. The paper will start to waver and distort. You can either leave the board with the paper on to dry at room temperature or, after five minutes, use a hair dryer to gently dry the paper. Leave the dry paper taped on the board and paint your picture on it, removing the picture at the end. Now the painting will be on a flat unwavering sheet of paper. I certainly recommend you stretch the first sheets of 90 lb (190gsm) and 140 lb (300gsm) paper as you prepare to work on them. Then, if you are not covering more than 50% of the paper with a painting, or not working wet, you can work on these papers without stretching them. The heavier weights of paper, from 260 lb (555gsm) upward, rarely need stretching.

Wet watercolor paper

Wipe edges

Tape down

Dry with hairdryer or at room temperature

Miscellaneous Materials

The materials listed below will be necessary to practice the demonstrations within this book.

Brushes:

1 x ½ in flat wash brush
1 x No. 10 round
1 x No. 6 round
1 x No. 4 round

Paints:

Alizarin Crimson
Ultramarine Blue
Cadmium Yellow
Payne's Grey
White Gouache
Burnt Sienna
Hooker's Green
Burnt Umber
Yellow Ochre
Cerulean Blue

Miscellaneous materials

Paper:

Sheets of watercolor paper — natural white

Optional items:

These items are readily available around the house or in an art supply store:

·   small genuine sponge
·   2 containers for water
·   a solid drawing board (ie: wood) about 18 x 14 in (460 x 350 mm)
·   scratch pad or scrap paper pad
·   soft tissues for blotting
·   bottle of black India ink and dip-in pen
·   masking fluid
·   toothbrush
·   tinted watercolor paper
·   2B pencil
·   kneaded putty eraser
·   gummed paper tape

Table easel

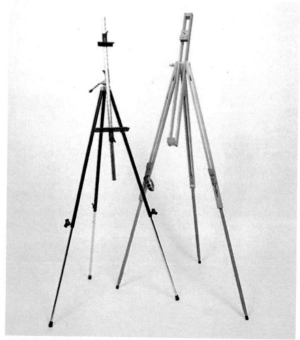

Sketching easels

Washes

It is a good idea to spend a few moments experimenting with your paints, paper and brushes to learn the different types of washes and how to apply them. This will help ensure your paintings looking fresh, clear and have the lovely translucent effect which is such a feature of watercolor painting.

A flat wash

This is just a mixture of water and color applied evenly. Use a round brush and mix water and a little Ultramarine Blue together on your palette. Apply brush strokes of the same length, letting each brush stroke touch the previous one. Do not rub or scrub with your paint brush. Do not go back over the brush strokes.

A graduated wash

Using your ½ in (13 mm) flat wash brush make a stronger mixture of Ultramarine Blue and water on your palette. Apply your first stroke from left to right and then add a little more water to the mixture and apply the second stroke to just touch the first stroke. Keep repeating this, reducing the mixture a little each time. Lightening a wash from dark to light, or adding color and darkening, has many uses in watercolor painting.

Hard edge and wet on wet washes.
Paint three strokes of Burnt Umber on the dry surface of your paper. The brush strokes stay just as you painted them. These are known as hard edge washes. Sometimes softer atmospheric effects are needed.

Wet the surface of your paper with a little clean water. Apply three similar brush strokes. The color will diffuse and spread. This is known as "wet wash" — wet paint on the surface of the wet paper or a wet painting. If you apply a watercolor wash onto a piece of newspaper, no matter how dark the wash, it should be translucent enough to see newsprint through it.

Brush strokes

Experiment with your round and flat brushes. Use them full of color and water, see how many different strokes you can create. Try them with very little water so that your brush seems to be running out of water. Brush strokes made with the brush like this are known as dry brush technique and have many uses. Try stippling, painting dots of color. Try gently jabbing your paint brush at the surface of the paper. You will be surprised just how many effects you can create.

Experiment... and have fun.

A flat wash   *A graduated wash*

Hard edge   *Wet on wet*

A wash on newsprint

Brush strokes

A graduated wash

Clouds lifted out with clean damp tissue

Color

Color Mixing

The practical and indispensable color charts on these pages help guide learning to mix colors.

The first chart shows how the three **Primary Colors**. red, yellow and blue, make the three Secondary Colors, orange, mauve and green. The **Secondary Colors** can be mixed to make the three Tertiary Colors, dark brown, light brown and olive green.

How to Make Black

Three primary colors mixed together produce black. I generally advise people not to use black paint to darken a color. It seems to dull and deaden the colors and they lose their clarity.

Complementary Color Wheel

black is opposite, or complementary, to white. Each color has its opposite color, shown on the *Complemetary Color Wheel* — black/white; yellow/mauve; orange/blue; red/green.

How to Make Gray

It is a good idea to ask yourself what is the predominant color of your subject and to try to have a splash of the opposite color in the painting. This can have a dramatic effect. If you mix any two opposite or complementary colors together in equal amounts, you produce grey.

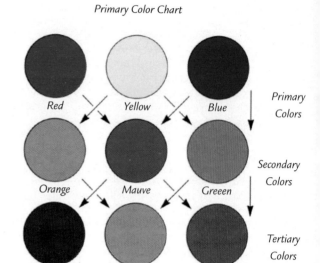

Primary Color Chart

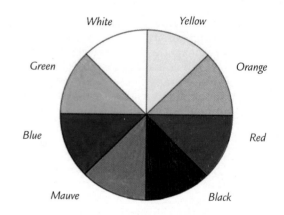

A Complemetary Color Wheel

14

The Color Tint Chart

Group your colors in the way I show. Paint a strong tone of the color in the first of the three boxes then make a medium tone made by adding a little white paint, then a light tone by adding even more white. This will show you the color and two of its lighter shades.

Greens Color Chart

This shows how with three blues, three yellows, one green, and white, you can make twenty-five greens all of value to anyone who paints, but especially to the landscape and floral painter. If you paint the charts on paper cut to A4 size, when dry, they can be placed in a clear plastic folder to keep them clean, ready for you to refer to when painting.

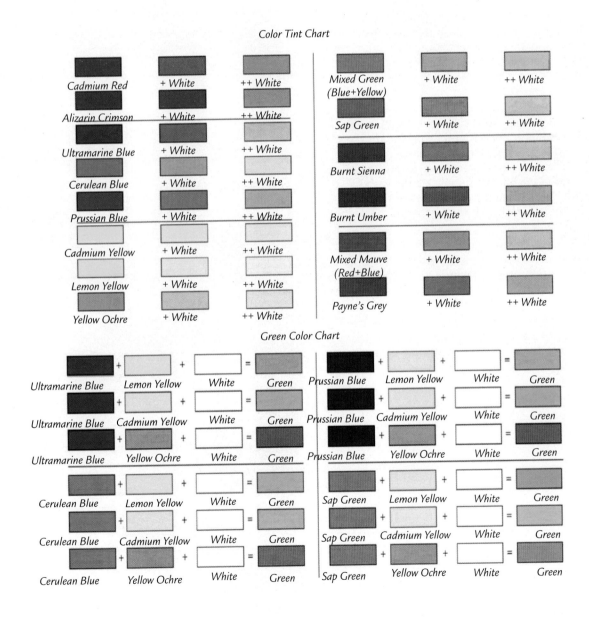

Color Tint Chart

Green Color Chart

Demonstration 1
Let's Paint a Picture

Throughout this book I will demonstrate a variety of subjects for you to try. A watercolor painting is normally built up by applying the lightest tones of each color, letting them dry, overlaying a second, layer of medium tones, and when dry adding the third, darker tones of each color. Finally the detail is added. This traditional technique is the best way to learn control of your watercolors and provide a good base on which to develop other techniques.

Stage 1 Stretch a piece of your watercolor paper measuring not less than 14 x 10 in (356 x 254 mm). When the paper is dry use your 2B pencil to sketch out the view as shown in this demonstration. Always decide where the light source is coming from to light your subject. We will imagine the sunlight is coming from the right hand side so the shadows will fall to the left.

Stage 2 Use a pale wash of Ultramarine Blue and apply the first wash for the sky with your largest round brush. Leave white paper showing for the white clouds. Use pale blue and mauve for the distant hills. Mix a pale green from Cadmium Yellow and Ultramarine Blue and apply a pale wash of green for the fields and tree foliage. Let these dry and add a pale wash of Burnt Umber to the path and tree trunk.

Stage 3 When dry, add a medium tone of each color to the areas you see in my stage three picture. Use a little less water and a little more color to make these medium tones. Leave some of the paler tones showing through.

Stage 4 When dry, add a darker tone to each area as in my stage four painting. The picture is beginning to build up. Now comes the part where everything falls into place.

Stage 5 Use a medium, or small, round brush and put in the details: the hedges detail to the tree trunk, boughs and branches, the fence, edges of the grass as it comes to the path, and, using a slightly dry brush with green on it, create a grass texture. Your painting should now be finished. Have a spare piece of paper at the side of your painting, so that as you mix your colors you can test them on the paper, before applying them to your painting.

Stage 1

Stage 2

Stage 3

Handy Hint: Have scrap paper at your side while you work so that as you mix your paints you can test them out before applying them to your picture.

Stage 4

Stage 5

17

Demonstration 2
Monochrome Lakeland Bridge

The understanding and application of tone in painting is of great importance. This aspect of painting is not difficult to understand. In Great Britain, during the Victorian period of the mid to late 1800s, art tutors were keen to encourage their students to understand tone by painting monochrome studies. Monochrome means mono (one), chrome (color): one color. They often used Sepia, a gentle brown color. While very few people I encounter today seem to be taught the techniques of monochrome painting I consider it an essential and very enjoyable aspect of learning to paint. It helps the development of fine painting skills. Try this demonstration of the Bridge House at Windermere in the English Lake District.

Stage 1 Lightly sketch out the subject using a 2B pencil.

Stage 2 Mix Burnt Umber with water to a pale tone and apply the first washes with your large and medium brushes. Let the washes dry.

Stage 3 Mix a medium tone of Burnt Umber and apply the washes of this tone as shown. Notice that in some areas the paler tone is left to show through. Let the washes dry.

Stage 4 Mix a darker tone of the color and apply the third tonal washes. Again, some of the paler and medium washes are allowed to show through as they become an important part of the painting. At this stage the painting should start to come together.

Stage 5 Use your smallest round brush and, with a fourth darker tone, created by using more color and less water, pick out and add details.

This technique is invaluable in the process of learning to paint successful watercolors. Look around you over the coming weeks and see how many examples of monochromes you can find. Black and white newspaper photographs, black and white television pictures, the blue willow pattern on china and many patterns and designs for bathroom and kitchen tiles are all examples of monochrome (one color in different tones) at work around you.

Handy Hint: Before you start your monochrome, use a spare piece of paper and mix the four tones of Burnt Umber and paint them onto the paper. Mix light, medium, dark and very dark. These can then be used to test each wash as you work, before applying the wash to the painting.

Stage 1

Stage 2

Stage 3

Stages 4 and 5, the details make the completed painting.

19

Demonstration 3
River Edge at Dawn

Watercolors can be applied to wet paper to create most appealing atmospheric background effects. To understand the dramatic effects which can be achieved we stay with monochrome painting but use a color called Payne's Grey. This is a strong, bluish grey. As we work with the paper very wet in areas, I suggest you stretch a piece of 140 lb paper.

Stage 1 Wet the top two thirds of your stretched paper with clean water. Leave the bottom third dry.

Stages 2 and 3 Mix Payne's Grey and water and drip it across the top of the wet paper. Pick your board up and quickly tip it from side to side, then tip it up vertically. Let the color spread.

Stage 4 Repeat stages 2 and 3 quickly while the sky is still damp. This should ensure the sky is darker at the top and paler as it comes lower down the page.

Stage 5 Following the above stages 1 to 4, your sky should look as shown here.

Stage 6 While the sky is damp use a pale tone of Payne's Grey and, with your No.10 or No.12 round brush, add the first stages and reflections of the reeds and the first effect of the river. Let the painting dry.

Stage 7 Now, using medium and darker tones of Payne's Grey and a No.3 round brush, use the traditional hard edge technique and add the tree, fence, birds, finished effects of the reeds, riverside bank and effects on the river. With the hard edge technique the brush mark or line stays where you place it. With the wet wash technique the color spreads and softens.

Stage 8 This is how the finished painting should look.

Watercolors dry by evaporation. If you are working wet and need an area to dry a little more quickly, you can use a hair dryer to speed up the process.

Stage 1

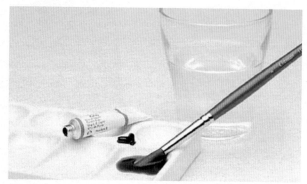

Stage 2

Stage 3

Stage 4

Stage 5

Stage 6

Stage 7

Stage 8

22

Sky and Cloud Techniques

It is often said the best things in life are free. We are surrounded by so many beautiful gifts of nature that it is easy to take them for granted. Nature's gifts are free for us to enjoy, and, for those of us who paint, to record for the enjoyment of others. When we look at a photograph the sky is static, frozen by the camera, unmoving. Yet stand for a few moments and look at the real sky, with clouds in it, on a gentle, sunlit day or a blustery, cold day. You will see the sky and clouds have a moving, ever changing nature. The skies of the four seasons, spring, summer, autumn and winter are so different. The height of the clouds, the strength of any prevailing wind, the varying strength of sunlight, the dryness or dampness of the day, all affect the sky. Nature offers the painter skies of tranquility and warmth to scenes of great drama. Skies are one of the greatest free shows on earth.

I show a series of demonstration skies which I suggest you try. These will help you explore the painting of skies and open up the possibilities skies offer to the landscape painter. They will help impart a freshness to your painting. Selecting just the right blue from your palette is important in achieving the right atmospheric effect. The blue for a hot summer's day is quite different from the blue required for a blustery autumn day.

I've shown a blues color chart which is well worth making out on a spare sheet of paper. As you look at your chart, look at the sky, plan to paint, or form part of your landscape, and achieve just the right coloring. I show how, if you have three blues, Ultramarine, Cerulean Blue and Prussian Blue, and paint three tones of each, you have nine blues and tints to select from. I also show how adding a small amount of Alizarin Crimson can make a mauvish blue, or a small amount of Burnt Umber can make a cool, greyish blue. I show how the paler tints of blue, with the addition of a small amount of Burnt Sienna, can make very gentle greys, ideal for the soft and medium greys found in billowy cumulus type clouds.

Make out the chart, and then use it to help paint the following sky demonstrations.

Blues Color Tint Chart

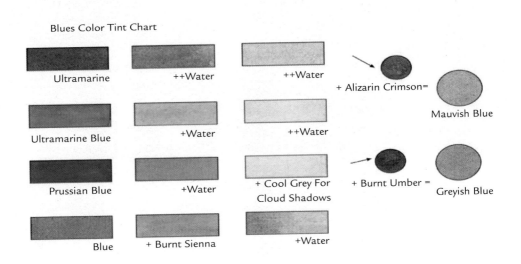

Demonstration 4
Lifting Out Clouds

This painting is of a gentle landscape, with light, billowy clouds coming up towards us from the horizon in a cool, blue sky.

Stage 1 Using your flat wash brush paint a graduated wash of Ultramarine Blue.

Stage 2 Crumple up a ball of clean, damp tissue. While the sky is still wet, dab and jab the damp tissue ball on the sky and it will create very convincing clouds.

Stage 3 Sketch in, and with your round brushes, paint the landscape. Note how the stronger tones of blue towards the top of the sky, and the stronger tones of green in the foreground of the fields help to create an illusion of distance, with the colors softening as they recede.

Stage 1

Stage 2

Stage 3

Demonstration 5
High Fleeting Clouds

This is the type of day when one wants to wear the lightest of shirts or blouses and to enjoy the warm sunlight. The sky has just a hint of fleeting clouds.

Stage 1 Apply a graduated wash of Cerulean Blue with your flat brush.

Stage 2 While the sky is still wet, use the ball of damp tissue technique described in the previous demonstration to lift out a few fleeting clouds in the way I show.

Stage 3 Let the sky dry. Sketch and paint in the landscape with your round brushes. Note how I use three tall poplar trees to help give the added effect of recession to the landscape

Stage 1

Stage 2

Stage 3

Demonstration 6
A Fused Colored Sky

Skies often have more than just one color in them. Some skies have clearly defined clouds and cloud masses, others can be hazy, atmospheric skies with no clouds, but with a variety of hints of colors within them. In this demonstration we use the wet wash technique as shown in the "River Edge at Dawn" demonstration, but with two colors in the sky.

Stage 1 Wet the top half of the page with clean water. Mix and brush in a little Cerulean Blue, leaving some areas of white paper.

Stage 2 As the color spreads, and while still wet, mix a little Alizarin Crimson. Touch a few brush marks of this color onto the wet blue sky. The colors will fuse and soften giving a delightful effect. Let the sky dry.

Stage 3 Sketch in and paint the lansdcape. Note how with the foreground lake I have picked up some of the reflected sky colors on the surface of the lake. I have also used a small fence on the left to help take the eyes into the picture from the left hand side.

Stage 1

Stage 2

Stage 3

Demonstration 7
A Storm At Sea

Now for a really dramatic sky. In this painting I use a little summer sky in the top right hand corner, but want to achieve the effect of a storm brewing up at sea, with the heavy nimbus-like clouds rising up from the left hand bottom corner and side of the horizon. It is the type of impending storm when any ship's captain would look for the nearest port or harbor.

Stage 1 Paint a pale wash of Cerulean Blue in the top right hand corner of the sky. Let it dry.

Stage 2 Using a large round brush, or a large flat brush, paint a medium tone wash of Prussian Blue from the left, just up to, and just over, the dry first stage. Let it dry. Then mix Prussian Blue with a little Burnt Umber to make the dark, heavier blue and paint the storm clouds upwards and across the sky from the left and the horizon.

Stage 3 Using pale and medium tones of Prussian Blue, paint in the sea, which should look as though it is just becoming choppy, leaving white flecks of paper to add to this effect. With a No.3 or No.6 round brush add the ship to the left of centre and the headland to the right on the horizon.

Stage 1

Stage 2

Stage 3

Demonstration 8
Niarbyl Bay — Isle of Man

What you leave out of a painting is as important as what you put in. I have had the enjoyment of painting and demonstrating in some of the most glorious and paintable locations on earth. One of my favourite locations is on the Isle of Man, on the west coast of England, just south of the town of Peel. It is Niarbyl Bay. A group of white cottages nestles beneath the cliffs just a few yards from the sea.

Although I painted this view from life, sitting at the bay, I did take some photographs so that you could see the original location and could see what I put in and what I left out. I left out the modern addition of the black and white building to the right of the cottages, the washing by the left of the door and the cars. I selected the angle of the cottages, but found by walking back some 20 metres .

I could use the small, curving sea wall and foreground grass on the right to add to the composition. The wall takes the eyes in, towards the cottages. The upturned boat was in the position you see and the seagull just happened to sit on the wall while I was painting. The figures were holiday makers who came to see what I was painting. I asked the father and son if they would go and stand in the spot you now see them and look out to sea so that I could paint them into the picture to add human interest.

A camera is a handy tool, artists can do more than the camera. The camera could not leave the washing out but I did.

This painting encompasses all I have so far taught you. If you try this demonstration, you should be well on the way to a real understanding of painting with watercolors.

Stage 1 Sketch out the subject lightly with a 2B pencil.

Stage 2 Using a large round or flat wash brush, paint in the first light washes for each area or item. The sky is a mixture of Ultramarine and Cerulean Blue. For the grass use Hooker's Green. For the cliffs use a mixture of pale Yellow Ochre and Burnt Sienna. For the sea use pale Ultramarine. The grey of the wall, roadway and grey cliff area are a mix of Ultramarine and Burnt Umber.

Stage 3 Build up the medium tones of each area and each item.

Stage 4 With your No. 3 or No. 6 round brush add the darker tones. Add the details to the thatch, rocks, sea, wall, grass, boat and figures.

While I encourage people to work from life whenever possible, often people wish to learn to paint indoors first, particularly if the weather is inclement. The demonstrations in this book will be of real help to you if you try them out. Now start to look through magazines, calendars and your own family photographs to see if you can find several subjects you could paint. This will allow you to try out the techniques you will have learned from my demonstrations. It will also enable your own individual style to start to show in your paintings.

Photographs of subject

Stage 1

Stage 2

Stage 3

Stage 4

Niarbul Bay
Texture Effects

Thatch

1. Paint a pale wash of Yellow Ochre.

2. Use our flat ½ in wash brush. Mix a darker tone of Yellow Ochre. Wipe the brush almost dry on some tissue. Press the brush down on spare paper so that the hairs become slightly splayed out. Pull the brush, following the slow of the thatch, to achieve the above texture.

3. Repeat stage two using Yellow Ochre with a little Burt Umber. Remember, keep the brush almost dry.

Cliffs & Rocks

1. Use pale Yellow Ochre with Burt Sienna for the warm areas. Paint a pale wash of Hooker's Green for the grass and a mix of Ultramarine and Burt Umber for the grey rocks.

2. Add the second tone for each area.

3. Add the third tone for each area and, with a fine brush, pick out and emphasize the craggy surface of the brownish cliff, grey rocks, and grass.

  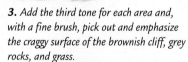 

Grass

1. Paint a pale wash of Hooker's Green.

2. When dry, mix a second tone of the green with a touch of Burnt Umber. Paint it on as shown. Let it dry.

3. Splay out a clean, medium-sized round brush in the same way as described for the thatch. Catch a deeper green on the brush tips. Pull the brush gently upwards and the grass texture will appear.

Demonstration 9
Tree Techniques

There are several mini demonstrations I like people to try key to learning to paint almost any type of tree.

You should always remember that trees are living, growing things. Most trees change with the season. Trees should always look as though birds could fly in and out of them. One should always be conscious of the general shape of the tree, its age, and the season that you are painting it in, spring, summer, autumn or winter. In the first tree demonstration panel below I show trees in their winter state, with no foliage.

Note with the younger of the two tree trunks how I use a round brush and paint the brush strokes upward from the ground and outward from the trunk. Trees grow upwards, not downwards. As the tree grows, each part of the trunk, boughs, and branches become thicker lower down and get thinner the higher or further away you get from the trunk and boughs. Always remember thicker getting thinner. Tree trunks, especially older tree trunks, can make marvellous subjects with great character. Try these two watercolor sketches and then see if you can find examples of your own to paint.

Tree trunks start thicker at the bottom and become thinner as they grow upwards. The same applies to boughs and branches.

Winter trees

Tree trunk textures vary widely and make good subjects to paint.

A fan brush can be used in a dry brush technique to create winter or summer trees, depending on the color of paint used.

Handy Hint: If there is a tree in your garden or near your home, paint it from life in each of the four seasons. It is amazing just how much this exercise can help you understand the nature of trees as you focus on the different details of the tree that become visible in each of the seasons.

Trees in Leaf

Use long curving strokes for trees like yew.

1 Basic shape of tree. **2** Light tones painted in. **3** Medium tones added. **4** Dark tones and details added.

Use dots for evergreens

Use short, semi-circular brush strokes for leafy trees.

Sponge technique

1 Light tones applied. Let them dry.

2 Medium tones and dark tones added with sponge. When dry, detail added with a brush.

Hedges can also be created with a sponge.

Around the Home

So far we have looked at landscape subjects. If you have tried the demonstrations you should already have learned some very useful techniques which can also be applied to a wide range of other subjects. You should also be gaining confidence in your own painting skills. Now look around you, around your home, in fact in the very room you are reading this book. You will find subjects all around you. Often the every day items we take for granted can make ideal subjects to sketch and paint. In my lounge is a trophy my daughter won for public speaking. In a kitchen cupboard I found an everyday coffee jug. Both proved interesting to paint. See if you can find one or two individual subjects you can try to paint from life. What I do strongly recommend is that you start to keep a watercolor sketch book. A medium sized spiral bound sketch pad, with 140 lb "**Not**" watercolor paper is ideal as you can flip the finished sheets over to reveal the next page,

yet all the pages remain intact in the spiral bound sketch pad. Just wander around your home looking for subjects and add a new subject to the sketch pad every day or so. Fruit, vegetables, ornaments, books, potted plants and fresh flowers, workbox tools, everyday objects provide a wealth of material for you to paint. Van Gogh painted a chair and a pair of boots. If he found this worthwhile it should commend itself to us also. Look for small objects like a key or watch and paint them up larger than life size. Try reducing some larger items to a smaller size. Experiment. This is a good way of introducing you to painting from life.

A Watercolor Sketchbook

Demonstration 10
Trawler — Watercolor and Pencil

There are a range of watercolor techniques including a little known one of combining watercolors and pencil. While the pencil is often used for sketching the subject out prior to painting, the pencil can be used on top of the finished watercolor to achieve a subtly different effect. In the demonstration of the trawler which I found in Peel Harbour on the Isle of Man, I show the traditional pencil sketch. On the right hand side of the sketch I have added the main watercolor washes. I did not add the finishing details with my paint brush, but used a 2B soft pencil to oversketch the painting, adding and emphasising the textures of the rocks, grass and detail of the trawler.

In the technique used for the trawler the whole subject is painted in watercolors, but another variation of the technique, which can make for highly distinctive studies is shown in the pencil and watercolor study of the tulip opposite. In this technique, the stem and leaves of the flower are sketched and shaded to a finished stage using a 2B pencil. The tulip head is painted in watercolor and oversketched in pencil. There is no reason why you should not mix the media in this way if it will give you the effect you seek. I have painted studies of birds in which the branch and foliage the bird is sitting on are in pencil, and the bird, the main subject of the picture, has been painted in watercolors. Always be prepared to experiment.

Stage 1

Stage 2

Stage 3

Demonstration 11
Tulip — Pencil and Watercolor

Try out both of the variations of the pencil and watercolor technique, adding them to your increasing repertoire of techniques you are now buiding up.

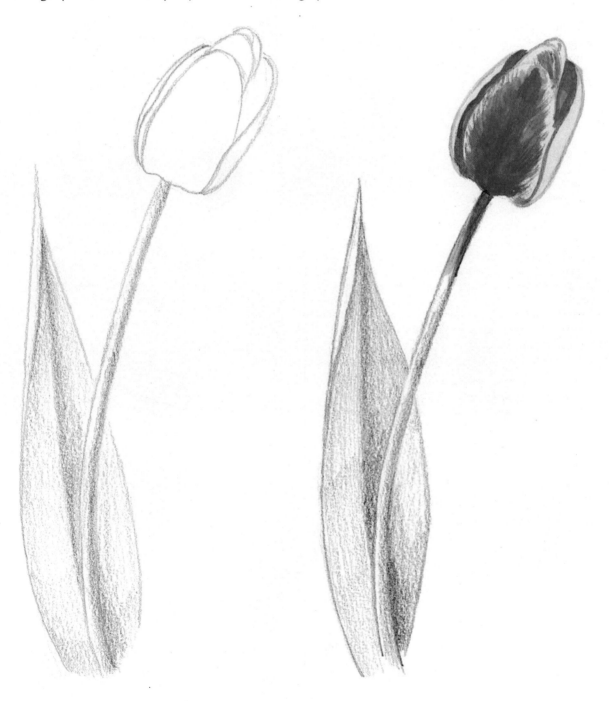

Stage 1 I picked this tulip from our garden. The stem and leaves are sketched out and finished using a 2B pencil. The tulip head is only lightly sketched out.

Stage 2 The tulip head is painted with watercolors and when dry over-sketched in pencil.

Pen and Wash

Pen and wash is one of the most enjoyable avenues of watercolor painting. It allows you to produce quick color sketches of subjects or finished art work. When nine years old I recall the class teacher telling the whole art class not to put black lines around everything. Children often do this to make things stand out, instead of using perspective and light and shade to achieve the same effect.

Pen and wash pictures are where the artist uses a black pen and ink, or a fine nylon or felt-tip pen, to over-sketch the subject to achieve a distinctive effect. Pen and ink usually refers to the use of a dip-in type pen with a metal nib together with a bottle of black waterproof India ink. It is possible to buy mapping pens and drawing pens singularly or in a set. These are obtainable from most art shops or stationers. I like the dip-in type nib. It allows you to vary the thickness of the line by altering the amount of pressure you apply to the pen. It allows for a considerable degree of expression of line on the artists part. It is possible to buy waterproof nylon or fine felt-tip pens which are wonderful to use in situations where it may not be convenient to use a dip-in pen and ink. Generally speaking, the ink in these pens is not light fast and can be subject to fading over a period of time if exposed to strong day light. India ink is permanent, waterproof and light fast.

There are a number of technical drawing pens on the market. These are used by architects and draughtsmen and many artists also enjoy using them. The line produced is the thickness of the nib used. Different thicknesses of nib are available and these are interchangeable.You can be inventive and use a cocktail stick or even sharpen a piece of bamboo cane. These all offer distinctive, individual types of mark or line.

This small sketch of Tuscany was produced in just five minutes. Quick outdoor sketches in this technique can provide original colored sketches, enabling the artist to paint larger, finished pictures from them in the studio if there has been insufficient time to paint the finished picture on location.

Demonstration 12
Water mill

I discovered this delightful water mill one summer's afternoon on a walk through a glen in the Isle of Man. Do not have too much ink on your dip-in pen nib. Too much ink can lead to blots. Test the pen nib each time you dip into the ink on a piece of scrap paper.

Stage 1 Sketch the subject out with a 2B pencil on 140 lb. "**Not**" watercolor paper.

Stage 2 Paint in the light, medium and dark tones for each area using the methods described in the earlier chapters of this book. Do not paint in the details. Leave the watercolor at the three quarters finished stage.

Stage 3 Use a dip-in pen, or a nylon or felt-tip pen, to over-sketch the subject. The result should be fresh, crisp and eye-catching.

Stage 2

Stage 1

Stage 3

Demonstration 13
Villa Pitiana - Tuscany

Many people have the opportunity each year to go on holiday. While the country we live in provides a wealth of subjects, the advent of modern forms of travel, especially air travel, offer us the opportunity to visit foreign countries, which in many instances our parents and grandparents could only read about or see photographs of.

On one occasion, I had the good fortune to hold one of my painting holiday courses at the Villa Pitiana in Tuscany, to the east of Florence. This 12th-century former palace, bathed in warm sunlight, offered the perfect subject for a pen and wash study. I used a sheet of 140 lb. HP, smooth watercolor paper. The colors used were Cerulean Blue, Hooker's Green, Yellow Ochre, Lemon Yellow, Ultramarine, Burnt Umber and Scarlet Lake.

Watercolor paper comes in three textures. "**HP**" Hot pressed, or smooth, is ideal for detailed work and pen and wash studies. "**Rough**" is not suited to pen and wash work. "**Not**" watercolor paper is neither rough nor smooth, but also lends itself to pen and wash work.

Stage 1 Sketch the subject out using a 2B pencil.

Stage 2 Paint in the sky using a wet wash technique with Cerulean Blue. Use the same pale blue on the olive trees.

Use a mix of pale Hooker's Green for the pale green area of foliage and fields. Paint a mix of the same green with a little Cerulean Blue added for the darker tones of the foliage behind the palace. Use Lemon Yellow with Hooker's Green for the right hand light tree. Use Hooker's Green with Ultramarine and Burnt Umber for the darker trees. Mix a little Yellow Ochre and Lemon Yellow for the painted wall plaster of the palace. Use Scarlet Lake and Lemon Yellow for the roof. A pale mix of Ultramarine and Burnt Umber will provide the pale grey of the stone walls and palace stone work. Paint a greyish blue from Ultramarine and Burnt Umber for the road.

Stage 3 Over-sketch with pen and ink.

Stage 1

Stage 2

Stage 3

Portrait on a Train

Left I was sitting on a train one day returning from Manchester to Southport, when at Wigan station this wonderful character, a workman who had just finished his shift, came and sat down on the seat across the aisle. I had my sketching materials handy and produced this felt-tip pen and wash sketch. His rugged face, work-worn hands and the dark browns and black of his clothes made him an exciting subject to paint. The speed of the felt-tip pen and wash method enabled me to sketch this in ten minutes, just before he reached his station and left the train.

A Doll

Below Most fathers of young daughters like to buy them dolls, and if they travel abroad they often bring back dolls in the national costume of the country they have been to. My daughter Penelope now has quite a collection. I came across this little fellow on a visit to Dallas and Houston. His impish smile and colorful clothes immediately caught my eye. He also shows that even children's toys can provide exciting material to paint. I sketched him out in pencil, added the colors, then used my fine felt-tip pen to over-sketch him.

Composition

The sketch or drawing of your subject, your skill in coloring it, the illusion of the textural effects, the use of light and shade, are all important elements of your painting. Equally important is the composition of a painting.

There are certain guide lines that, if followed, can help build a sound compositional foundation for your work. One important rule is to not have any line or object cut your picture into two equal halves in order to avoid monotony in the composition. Note how in Views A and B below, the views are cut in half horizontally by the horizon and vertically by the tree trunk. By setting the horizon slightly lower (View C) and offsetting the tree trunk to the left of center (View D) the composition becomes much more dynamic and visually interesting.

Focal points and key lines

When looking at your work, the viewer's eyes should not be wandering around the sketch as though lost. You are the artist; you are in control, so decide what it is that you want people to be looking at in particular. In other words, your picture should have a **focal point**, or a main feature to which the eyes are led.

In View E, the focal point is the barn, set in the distance. In View F, it is the castle in the far distance, and in View G it is the shed in the foreground.

I have arrowed the **key lines** in each view as well so that you can see how the details in the pictures follow these key lines and lead the viewers eye to the focal points helping to bring the entire composition together.

View A   Halfway

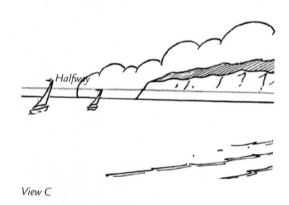

View C

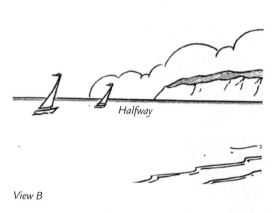

View B   Halfway

View D   Halfway

View E

View F

View G

The Triangle

A triangular composition can offer an excellent shape on which to base a painting, especially a landscape, still life or floral study. In the three illustrations, View H, I and J, I show this at work. In H, a still life is created from a wine bottle, wine glass, bowl of fruit and bananas. I have placed the wine bottle to the left, forming the left side of the triangle, and the bottom of the glass, bowl of fruit and bananas form the base of the triangle. In I, the shape of the bowl holding the fruit adds to the triangular format of this subject, with the apex just off-center to the right. In J, the triangular shape of the vase containing the flowers helps add to the triangular format of the composition.

Try to ensure that still life and floral studies have height, width and depth to them.

The next time you have the opportunity to look at paintings or prints by any of the great masters, or even by any fine artist of today, look closely to see how they have employed the important compositional points I have referred to here.

View H

View I

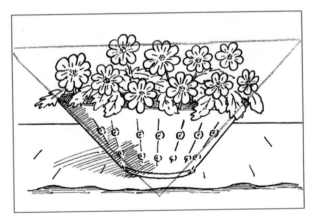

View J

45

Perspective

The **Horizon line** is an imaginary line across your field of vision when you look straight on; not up or down, but straight ahead. In my sketch you see how the horizon line stays directly in front of the subject regardless if he is sitting down, standing level, or standing higher on a dune. To determine the horizon line when looking at a real subject, hold a ruler by its thin side, horizontally in front of your eyes. This is where the horizon line should be in your composition. Generally, I suggest that you draw the subject lightly first, though, then apply your horizon line to your sketch. Your horizon line is then used to help apply perspective to the rest of your work and to check and correct your subject.

Perspective is a system of creating the illusion of three dimensions in the objects in your sketch. One way to see perspective in action is to picture the view looking down railroad tracks. The rail ties appear to become smaller and closer together until the tracks merge and disappear.

The point where the tracks appear to merge is the "**Vanishing Point**" (VP), which you will note is a point on the Horizon Line. We know that they don't merge in reality, however by having them vanish on the horizon line we create the illusion that they are getting further away and that the scene has depth.

Below My sketch illustrates this, and I show the tracks with three trees to the right, and then also with telephone poles to the left. Both the trees and the poles appear to become smaller and closer together as they recede. I have shown the guidelines for each item, illustrating how the guidelines all meet at the vanishing point on the horizon line.

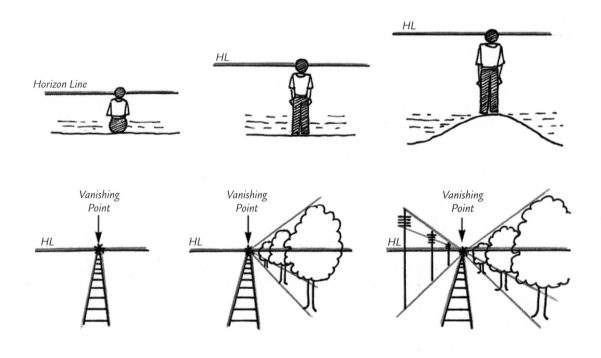

Next I show a front view of a normal dinning room chair. With this view there is just one vanishing point on the horizon line for the sides of the seat and for the base lines of the legs. I am imagining that you or I would be sitting on a chair of similar height when drawing this chair, in which case, I think you would find your eye level would be just about 18 in (46cm) above the back of the chair. In my next sketch the chair is set at an angle. We now have two vanishing points, one for each side of the chair. Guidelines will often converge at eye level, but off the page. This is quite normal and often happens. When it does, lay scrap paper at the side and tape it on from behind, then extend the guidelines onto it, in the way I show in my sketch. Never guess or assume the perspective is correct, always try to "prove" it.

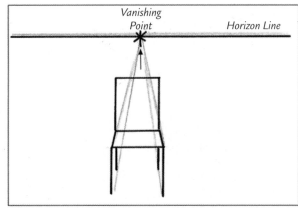

Chair front on

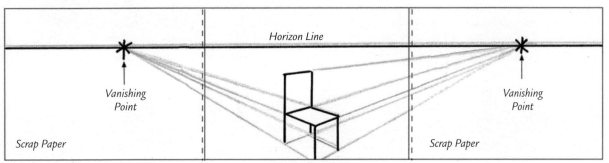

Chair at an angle

Circular Perspective

Few people realize that perspective can be used to help solve the problems of drawing circles and ellipses, but it can. I have illustrated this in a sketch of a wine bottle and two glasses, one on its side. I have lightly drawn the group out and placed my eye level well above it. I have then drawn a light guiding square around each ellipse and have drawn those squares in perspective, in the same way the basket was drawn. The squares for the ellipses each have their perspective vanishing points on the common eye level. The ellipses for the glass on its side are on a different plane so they have their own vanishing point at a different position on the eye level. The use of the squares helps determine where each vanishing point should be and ensures the true perspective of the subject where there is an ellipse involved. I then go back to each ellipse and check that it touches the center of each side of the square it occupies, for provided it does, I know that the ellipse must be in perspective. The squares used outside each ellipse and perspective guidelines can be rubbed out gently before a picture is shaded or painted.

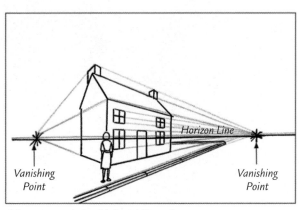

A house at an angle with 2 vanishing points

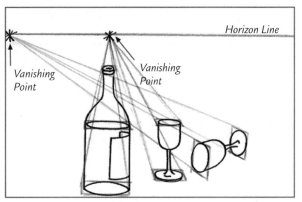

Circular perspective. Wine bottle and two glasses

Demonstration 14
Masking Fluid

Masking is a water-based rubber solution used to protect an area of paper, allowing you to paint in a later stage. To show the effects you can achieve using masking fluid, I've shown a duck on a lake. If I simply drew the duck and painted the lake water up to it, the duck would look painted up to, and not have the effect of the water being in front, around, and behind.

Stage 1 Sketch out the duck.

Stage 2 Use masking fluid to cover the shape of the duck. Let the masking fluid dry.

Stage 3 Paint the lake effect over the duck, ignoring it. When the washes are dry, gently rub the masking fluid with a clean fingertip and the masking fluid will peel away, leaving the white duck to be painted in.

Do not let the masking fluid dry on your brush, keep washing it off while still wet. Do not use a hair dryer to dry the watercolor if using masking fluid. Practise using masking fluid on some spare watercolor paper before using it in a painting.

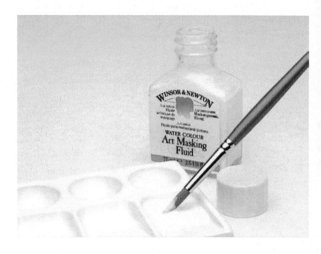

Stage 1

Stage 2

Stage 3

Demonstration 15 & 16
Gouache

There are water based colors known as gouache, designers colors or poster colors. These are opaque water based colors. During the past century, some artists, such as the great English painter Turner, described them as "Body Color". If painted on newspaper, or colored paper, the paint obliterates the newsprint or colored paper due to the paints opaqueness. Watercolors are translucent. This is one of the medium's most distinctive features. To experiment with gouache you do not have to buy a set of gouache paints, because by adding permanent white gouache to your watercolors you can make them opaque. Only add enough water to make the paint mixture flow freely off the brush. Do not dilute it as much as for normal watercolor painting.

An excellent way to arrive at the right degree of opacity for gouache is to try painting the cup below on a piece of newspaper, using permanent white and Prussian Blue watercolor mixed together. Add a little Burnt Umber to the blue for the darker tones. Use the technique described over the page.

To discover the difference between watercolors and gouache, paint the tree shown using the normal watercolor technique on watercolor paper with no white paint. Then try the tree in the gouache technique on a piece of tinted paper. Watercolors should be translucent, gouache should be opaque.

Above Tree. Watercolor

Below Tree. Gouache

Demonstration 17
Gouache – Wine Bottle

Here is a simple demonstration of a wine bottle for you to try. I use a piece of maroon paper to achieve my effect; I think it is well worth buying some the next time you are in an art supply store.

Stage 1 Draw out the subject. Mix the pale green from Hooker's Green watercolor and permanent white gouache. Paint the label white.

Stage 2 Mix medium and darker tones of green for the bottle by adding a little Ultramarine and Burnt Umber to the Hooker's Green on your palette. For the label add a pale grey shadow. Add the table cloth using permanent white gouache and Prussian Blue.

Stage 3 Mix the light yellowy greens and highlights by adding a little Lemon Yellow and white to the Hooker's Green and paint these on. Add the shadow for the bottle and the lines on the table cloth. Finally add a hint of detail to the bottle label.

Demonstration 18
Painting on Tinted Watercolor Paper – Sunset

Watercolor paper has traditionally been white to allow the light to be reflected back through the washes applied on it. However I have often been intrigued by the possibility of, and have experimented with, tinting my watercolor paper all over with a color, then painting my watercolor on that tinted paper surface. I show two demonstrations that not only open up this possibility for you, but that helped persuade a major English watercolor paper manufacturer to produce and extensively market tinted watercolor papers.

Stage 1 Mix a wash of pale Yellow Ochre. Apply it with your flat wash brush. Let it dry thoroughly.

The first demonstration is a lakeland sunset.

Stage 2 Mix a graduated wash of Alizarin Crimson. Apply the wash from dark to light from the top, and light to dark from the middle to the bottom. Let it dry.

Stage 3 Paint in the middle distance hills and the same shapes reflected in the lake. As you come to the darker tones add a little Payne's Grey to the Alizarin Crimson.

Stage 4 Paint in the boats moored at anchor and the foreground grasses on the nearside of the lake.

Handy Hint: It is essential that the color used to tint the paper is absolutely dry before you paint over it. Use a hair dryer to speed the drying of the paint on the paper.

Stage 1

Stage 2

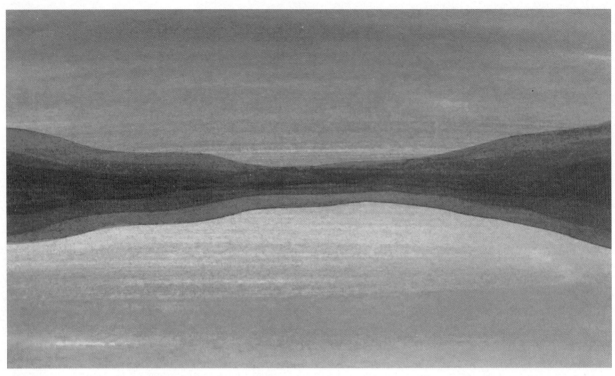

Stage 3

Stage 4

Demonstration 18
Painting on Tinted Watercolor Paper – River View

Part of the fun of painting is to experiment. The medium is as flexible as your imagination. If it surprised you to find me suggesting you used Alizarin Crimson over Yellow Ochre, let me surprise you even further by suggesting you try Hooker's Green over Yellow Ochre.

Stage 1 Paint a wash of pale Yellow Ochre and let it dry.

Stage 2 Mix a wash of Hooker's Green and paint an upward curving graduated wash, darker at the top, paler in the middle. Then paint a paler, downward graduated wash, becoming darker at the bottom. Let it dry.

Stage 1

Stage 2

Stage 3 Use a darker tone of the green, paint in the first stages of the trees, island and the river banks.

Stage 4 Mix a little Payne's Grey with the Hooker's Green to make a darker tone, add the details to the trees and boat mooring post. Use the dry brush technique to finish the effects of the grasses in the areas one show. When you have learned and mastered the basic foundations of watercolor painting, develop an adventurous nature, be prepared to throw caution to the wind and experiment with the medium; you could be surprised at the results.

Handy Hint: When you have learned and mastered the basic foundations of watercolor painting, develop an adventurous nature; be prepared to throw caution to the wind and experiment with the medium. You could be surprised at the results!

Demonstration 20
Figures

Many people enjoy landscape painting but shy away from adding figures for fear of spoiling the paintings. Figures add human interest and can play an important role in good picture making. It is well worth practising figures on some spare paper to develop a practical approach to painting them.

Figures come in three main groups, foreground figures, middle distance figures and far distant figures. The middle distant figures are the ones you may find most useful. Below I show how to paint static and moving figures. There are many locations where you can practise sketching and painting real, live people. Bus and train stations, markets, cafes and seaside beaches offer a whole host of subjects. If you are unable to go out of doors, thumb through magazines and find examples of the type and size of people I have demonstrated, and practise painting them.

Stage 1 Keep them simple. Sketch the male and female figures out in pencil. Draw a simple head, chest, pelvis and guide lines for the arms and legs.

Stage 2 Make the arms and legs more defined and add the clothes.

Stage 3 Use a medium sized brush and paint a medium wash of color for each part of the figure.

Stage 4 Use a smaller brush and paint a darker tone of each color for the areas of the figures in shadow.

Moving figures need to look fluid, not rigid. Again, success comes from keeping them simple. In the following demonstration I show a man in a rain coat blown along by the wind and rain, with his umbrella blown inside out The approach is exactly as in the four stages described below. Do not put in too much detail.

Stage 1   Stage 2   Stage 3   Stage 4

Stage 1   Stage 2   Stage 3   Stage 4

Demonstration 21
Still Life

Just as styles of handrwriting vary from one person to another, so do styles of painting. A painting by Constable has a very definite and unmistakable look. Leonardo da Vinci's style was totally different to Raphael's, but they were all great masters of painting. In this still life demonstration I show a looser technique for painting with watercolors. Instead of sitting down to paint this at a table I stood up. Standing encourages a looser approach and dramatically reduces the temptation to include unnecessary details.

Stage 1 The group was set up and drawn out using a triangular composition. The light comes from a window on the right of the picture.

Stage 2 I set a time limit of 15 minutes so worked quickly. I painted in the light and medium tones with my ½ in (13mm) flat wash brush and my No. 10 round brush.

Stage 3 I added the darker tones with the point of my No. 10 round brush.

Stage 2

Stage 1

Stage 3

Stage 4 Finished still life. Using my No. 6 round brush I added the key dark details to the wine bottle, glass, pineapple and lines of the check tablecloth.

Handy Hint: Try this demonstration, if possible, standing up. Then set a group of objects of your own choosing and paint that standing up.

Demonstration 22
Silhouettes – Palm Tree

Back lighting, where the lighting comes from behind the subjects, can be dramatic, as in a sunset. Back lighting can also offer silhouette opportunities. The objects in such pictures appear to lose their natural color and become very dark. While silhouettes often look black, my advice for silhouettes in a painting is to mix a very dark color from Alizarin Crimson, Ultramarine and Payne's Grey so that the resulting silhouettes are very dark,

but have a hint of subtle tonal variations in them, not looking like flat, cut out, paper shapes produced when using black paint. Paint a piece of watercolor paper with Lemon Yellow. Let it dry. Overpaint it with orange and then use Alizarin Crimson, Ultramarine and Payne's Grey mixtures to create the tropical sunset with silhouetted palm trees.

Stage 1

Stage 2

Stage 3

Stage 4

Demonstration 23
Painting with a Toothbrush

Even the humble toothbrush can play a part in painting. Let us stay with the idea of a sunset and use a different technique in a different demonstration.

Stage 1 Place a medium size coin in position to mask out the shape of the sun. Mix Lemon Yellow and press your toothbrush in the yellow paint. Hold the brush 3 in (75 mm) above the coin and flick the paint off the toothbrush with your finger by quickly pulling your finger towards you across the toothbrush. Let the paint dry.

Stage 2 Repeat stage one using Alizarin Crimson, but create a circle of splattered red paint about 2 in (50 mm) out from the coin by moving your toothbrush away from the coin and flicking round in a circle.

Stage 3 Use India ink and a fine brush to paint in the landscape subject.

Not only is it fun to do, but this is a technique I often use to make greeting cards as the technique can be adapted to a wide range of subjects.

Stage 1

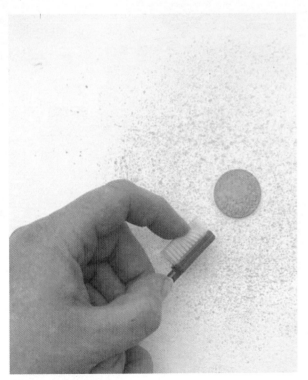

Stage 2

Stage 3

Painting From Photographs
Using a Camera

Some people frown on the use of a camera and painting from photographs. I believe a camera is a useful tool and can be helpful to the artist. Often when out, due to the shortage of time or the transitory nature of the subject, there may not be time to paint a picture. Take a photograph and use that as the basis for a painting. Another occasion you may see a subject and have time to make a quick sketch. If you also take a photograph you can work from the photograph and sketch in your studio, or at home, to produce your own original painting. I show a sketch below which I did in a boat yard. I took a photograph of the subject for added reference. This combination provided everything to produce a finished painting in my studio.

The colors in a photograph are not 100% accurate. They are a guide for you when painting. Sometimes a part, or a section, of the photograph will make a good subject in its own right. You are in charge, you can select, adapt and use a photograph to create the picture you want. Do not become a slave to photographs but they are a useful aid in the art of painting.

Picture Shapes

Most artists paint their picture up to the edge of their rectangular paper or painting surface. When you see such paintings in an exhibition they often look like postage stamps in an album. Experiment with picture shapes, don't let them become boring. Lay a tea or dinner plate face down on a piece of paper, draw around it, remove the plate and you have a circular format for a painting. Draw a round the top half of a plate to make a semicircle. Add straight sides and a straight baseline and you have another exciting shape to paint in. Buy an oval mount from an art shop.

Lay it on the paper to see the possibilities of a horizontal or vertical painting shape. Try tall, thin paintings and long, thin paintings.

Using a variety of shapes will not only add to your enjoyment of painting, but will often enhance the chance of work being accepted for exhibitions as it adds variety to the standard rectangular shapes so often submitted.

A variety of possible picture shapes

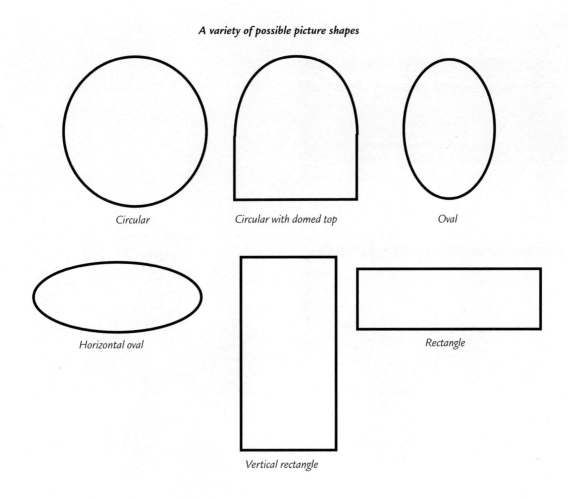

Circular   Circular with domed top   Oval

Horizontal oval   Rectangle

Vertical rectangle

Framing Watercolors

The framing and visual presentation of a watercolor is very important. Watercolors are normally framed, mounted, and placed under glass. The color of the mount chosen not only provides a complementary surround, but also provides an air space between the picture and the protective glass.

Generally I would say that if the painting is light use a darker mounting, if the painting is dark in color and tone use a lighter one.

Try to avoid diffused glass. Although this can take away the reflections of the light on glass it tends to grey the picture and one loses some of the freshness and detail of the work it covers.

While some people like to make their own frames, it is possible to buy very good, inexpensive, ready made frames and mounts from many retail outlets. You can also use the services of a specialist picture framer who will have an extensive range of frames and mount boards. He or she will almost certainly be pleased to help and advise you, and mount and frame your watercolor for you. This is a personal service like having a suit or dress made for you. The framer's service and expertise will be reflected in the price.

A mount and frame should enhance and complement a painting, not dominate it. You want people to remember the painting, not the frame.

Cross section of frame

Selling and Exhibiting Your Work

There are three unforgettable painting experiences: when you complete your first painting, when you sell your first painting and when you have one of your paintings hung for the first time in an exhibition.

Many people like to paint for their own enjoyment and also enjoy producing paintings to give to family and friends. However, it can be well worth enquiring at local libraries, art galleries and art shops where you live to see if the staff knows of any upcoming exhibitions you can enter work into. You can also find information in national art magazines on exhibits that they review or sponsor. Be sure to send for exhibition details as early as possible and read the instructions carefully as details and rules vary from one exhibition to another. Some exhibitions accept all work submitted, but limit the number of paintings people may enter, while others have selection committees. Sometimes it can be disheartening if a selection committee does not accept your work; but do not get discouraged. Often, due to the shortage of space or because of the sheer volume of work submitted, some excellent work is rejected. There is no reason you can't resubmit your work the next year or to other shows, so do try again.

Local hotels, restaurants and coffee shops often allow local artists to show their work on their premises. Local furnishing shops and commercial art galleries also will often welcome

the opportunity to show new work. Most towns and cities have art clubs and societies that can be well worth joining and tehey also stage members' exhibitions. Your local art shop or library will generally have details of the names and addresses of secretaries of local clubs and societies.

Handy hint: One thing to remember is that while copying paintings is a time honored way of learning to paint, do not exhibit or sell copies of other artists work, as this is, in certain instances an infringement of copyright.

Techniques and Advice

- Do use good quality art materials and look after them with care.

- Do paint subjects that inspire you.

- Do use two jars of water when painting watercolors, one to wash you brush in and one for clean water to mix with your paint.

- Do vary the sizes of your paintings: small, medium and large.

- Do experiment by painting a wide range of different subjects.

- Do not forget to replace caps on tubes of paint.

- Do not let finished watercolor paintings become soiled or damaged. Keep them in a portfolio.

- Do not forget to go outside and paint if at all possible./

- Do not use diffused glass when framing watercolors.

- Do not hesitate to enjoy your painting.

Remember... if you have ever said "I wish I could paint" my message to you is

If You Want To ... You Can!